RE

OTHER BOOKS FROM THE EMMA PRESS

THE EMMA PRESS PICKS

The Flower and the Plough, by Rachel Piercey
The Emmores, by Richard O'Brien
The Held and the Lost, by Kristen Roberts
Captain Love and the Five Joaquins, by John Clegg
Malkin, by Camille Ralphs
DISSOLVE to: L.A., by James Trevelyan
The Dragon and The Bomb, by Andrew Wynn Owen
Meat Songs, by Jack Nicholls
Birmingham Jazz Incarnation, by Simon Turner
Bezdelki, by Carol Rumens

POETRY PAMPHLETS

Paisley, by Rakhshan Rizwan
Elastic Glue, by Kathy Pimlott
Dear Friend(s), by Jeffery Sugarman
Poacher, by Lenni Sander
priced out, by Conor Cleary
The Stack Of Owls Is Getting Higher, by Dawn Watson
A warm and snouting thing, by Ramona Herman
The Whimsy of Dank Ju-Ju, by Sascha Aurora Akhtar
Vivarium, by Maarja Pärtna

POETRY ANTHOLOGIES

Some Cannot Be Caught: The Emma Press Book of Beasts
In Transit: Poems of Travel
Everything That Can Happen: Poems about the Future
The Emma Press Anthology of Contemporary Gothic Verse

REQUIEM

Mourning poems by Síofra McSherry
Illustrations by Emma Dai'an Wright

THE EMMA PRESS

For my mother.
What is remembered lives.

ℭ

THE EMMA PRESS

First published in the UK in 2019 by the Emma Press Ltd

ISBN 978-1-912915-40-8

A CIP catalogue record of this book
is available from the British Library.

Printed and bound in the UK
by Oxuniprint, Oxford.

The Emma Press
theemmapress.com
hello@theemmapress.com
Jewellery Quarter, Birmingham, UK

CONTENTS

Note: This sequence roughly follows the structure of the Requiem Mass. Phrases and quotations not in English are glossed at the back.

1. INTROITUS

AD TE OMNIS CARO VENIET

To you all flesh shall come
and before you all flesh shall cave.
Witness the bleed-out
of desire, the avalanche of synapses,
the extinction of the will. Unprepared
we shall wake to your all-blinding light,

we who carried flashlights and thought
we knew the sun. Your veils
shall set fast our limbs,
swaddle our mouths and noses, our eyes
and ears and skin. We shall speak nothing,
hear nothing, see nothing. Nothing shall be known.

Before you sense is scattered and meaning lies in ruin.
Before you come none willingly
and from you shall go none.
Hear our prayer.

2. KYRIE

KYRIE ELEISON
CHRISTE ELEISON

Lord have mercy upon her
Christ have mercy upon her
Day have mercy upon her
Night have mercy upon her

Bed have mercy upon her
Hoist have mercy upon her
Catheter have mercy upon her
Needle have mercy upon her

Gastrostomy have mercy upon her
Citalopram have mercy upon her
Riluzole have mercy upon her
Morphine have mercy upon her

Neurone have mercy upon her
Tendon have mercy upon her
Atrophy have mercy upon her
Phlegm have mercy upon her

Bladder have mercy upon her
Bowel have mercy upon her
Breath have mercy upon her
Heart have mercy upon her

3. GRADUALE

REQUIEM ÆTERNAM DONA EIS, DOMINE

Merry meet by forest road, by the smack of the side of
a bus or pearl nurtured in the shell of my own breast. .

Merry meet by blade or bullet, or the light of a sputtering
neurone. You are never far, nor hard to find.

I offer flowers to my body that will die.

I imagine us someday sitting creased and greyed on the
stoop together, rolling tobacco and reckoning scores,
but today I am here to look you in the eye, and live.

4. TRACT

ABSOLVE, DOMINE,
ANIMAS OMNIUM FIDELIUM DEFUNCTORUM
AB OMNI VINCULO DELICTORUM.

The odd unbustling Wednesday
in the Faithful Departed, the craic
will be spooling nicely when – with
little warning but a rash of goose-
bumps and a zebra shadow casting
to the bar – in he'll gangle. There's
ones that've had a bad run with him;
Orpheus got drunk and lost his
grip on the subject entirely, later
being ripped apart by women. *Il a
perdu son Eurydice*; he caved in
to his pain. A melancholic fellow,
that, not like *himself*, all clatter
and tooth, as generous with his grins
as with all else. Cora tends to the wipe
and sparkle with a necromantic glint
and the garden of their talk grows
steady and blooming. Oftentimes we'll
reach across and grab a pomegranate
seed or three when proffered, why not,
best to keep half an eye on where
we're headed, after all it's a rickety
bar-room this to wait out our time in.

5. SEQUENTIA

DIES IRÆ, DIES ILLA
SOLVET SÆCLUM IN FAVILLA,
TESTE DAVID CUM SIBYLLA.

All the world to wild Cassandra's
bloody vision presently conforms. Grey

ash clouds hang above the cities. David snorts some
coke before he goes on air to say these

circumstances were foreseen, and those who
live according to the Law should never

fear the Judge. The sky cracks open.
Heaven's gates break orbit as a hundred

million trumpets flare at once, and then fall
silent. All the world stands waiting, staring

upward. In the emptied-out saloon Death sits and
pours himself a double shot of rum, and

sighs. *This fucking guy.* The earth and oceans vomit
out the dead of sixty million years to face their

Maker's passiflora maw. He peels back the ozone layer,
turns out all the stars. In darkness scrolling

text appears, wrought in piercing light. It lists the
sins of all the world, since we were torn from

mud and algae and set to worship. We close our
eyes but see it scrolling still, in black on lidded red. Ellen

Mullen cheated on her husband, June of nineteen
ninety-four. Muhammad on the second floor

stole his neighbours' WiFi. Tor of Viken killed his father
with a poisoned cup the year of the good harvest.

Excuses have no meaning; all will be revealed.
Look what you just made me do. Death grimly

pours another drink. Outside, the desperate
corpses call on him. 'Great Death, save us from

Judgement! Death is a fountain of mercy,
gives freely, and ends all. We seek the gentle

ministry of worm, blowfly and beetle.
From paradise we were untimely ripped.'

Others call on Christ, and prompt the Lord to keep his
promise. *Even if the kid shows up, good luck finding*

Him in this shit-storm. The planet's surface reddens with
justice. Human, plant, and animal together

scream in supplication; remind the Judge that
others have been spared – what of Mary, unmarried

mother of the Lord? By all reports, she's queen of
heaven now. Likewise the thief – crucified, but

saved by the side of Christ. Exceptions have been
made. If the Judge but wills it we shall walk today in

paradise. What greater power has a god, than
to discriminate? Look! Our prayers, although unworthy,

have been heard. The circle of the righteous starts to
gather in a pool of widening light. Within it stand the

sheep; without, the goats, who wail and gnash their
teeth in everlasting pain. My heart is crushed to ashes.

Crawling and weeping, I drag myself into the light.

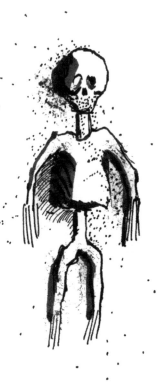

6. OFFERTORIUM

HOSTIAS ET PRECES, TIBI,
DOMINE, LAUDIS OFFERIMUS

The attributes of death are
aconite; laburnum;
a maguey worm; a smashed
iPhone; zero kelvin;
a broken accordion; a used
condom; a lost chess piece;
an unlabelled CD-ROM;
a taxidermied lark;
Channel 4 News; a 50,000
lira note; an unravelled
sweater; pencil shavings;
an unclouded mirror; that
which is ungiven and that
which is unreceived; an empty
glass; burned bread; you.

7. BENEDICTUS

BENEDICTUS QUI VENIT IN NOMINE DOMINI!

Death neither crept nor slithered when he came
nor routed us in battle; to us was offered neither
gunpowder nor plot, dulce nor decorum. He just
came in one day without knocking, nodded to us,
hung his hat in the hall, and left.

For the next few weeks we side-eyed
the black Borsalino hanging stiff
and dusty on the coat rack among our
summer jackets and raincoats in kingfisher,
cream, suede, and emerald green, as we passed
on our way out down the town.

We considered this behaviour ill-mannered.
The black hat shifted the symmetry of things, made
us feel on edge without quite knowing why.
The geometry of the house changed. The paths
between rooms we'd known for twenty years
suddenly switched around. A bed appeared
in the sitting room for the times Flower
couldn't make it up the stairs.

Death took to visiting more often. He tended
to lurch alarmingly as if he might fall, but somehow
maintained an exasperating swagger. His legs were thin
as candy canes and his jaw was startlingly defined.
He made us feel awkward and we wished his visits
were shorter. We could never think of anything to say.
To make things worse we kept finding things he'd left
in every room, empty bottles of cheap imported
beer, a pack of playing cards with all the queens
missing, an annotated copy of Pope's *Essay on Man*,
papier-mâché Día de los Muertos figurines that clashed
with the décor, which was mostly magnolia
and terracotta, a country farmhouse theme, with oak.

Not knowing Death's address we put the things
out at the edge of the drive, but they reappeared
on the fireplace and the coffee table overnight.
Growing annoyed and feeling somewhat taken
advantage of we drove the stuff to the dump in a quite
clear statement that we and dust were done;
the next day, however, they returned.

We have grown accustomed to tripping
over nonsense in the hall. Memento mori
bob in the bath with us and nestle
on our pillows when we wake. The deluge
takes its toll on our good will, although
we try to remain hospitable. Flower broke
down crying the other night after emptying the oven
of stained artificial daffodils only to find the fridge
was full of spiders. Some days it takes an hour
to dig the car out of the dirt.

We don't go out much anymore. Flower
has taken permanently to bed in the front
room and the things she says grow further
and further apart. We find your intrusion
at this time to be particularly inconvenient.

8. AGNUS DEI

AGNUS DEI QUI TOLLIS PECCATA MUNDI,
DONA NOBIS PACEM.

For a year I watched the woman who bore me wane.
She was a sweet-voiced mahogany guitar
until sickness cut her strings. One by one
her chords diminished until a voiceless box remained
that laughed and choked and wept in silence.

My aunts strung together rosaries to hang
across the silence, as they did while Carmel died,
and Brigid, Joseph, Mary, and James. Gentle
lamb, who takes away the sins of all the world,
speak; tell us why you too are silent.

9. COMMUNION

LUX PERPETUA LUCEAT EIS, QUIA PIUS ES.

May you be illuminated always.

Your nails were a perfect crescent moon of white on pink. Your
forehead smelled like freesias when you kissed me goodnigh

You starred as a young woman in *My Fair Lady* but I never hear
you sing it. I used to think you sang too loudly in church.

May an inexhaustible spotlight pick you ever out.

You knew the name of every plant in each of your three
gardens. You knew how to murder greenfly.

To be honest, I've already lost your voice and most of your face,
rank and file now with the massed dead.
No name I know can call you.

Seht ihr's nicht?
Immer lichter wie er leuchtet,
stern-umstrahlet hoch sich hebt?

10. LIBERA ME

TREMENS FACTUS SUM EGO, ET TIMEO,
DUM DISCUSSIO VENERIT, ATQUE VENTURA IRA.

What element do you call home now? All your
grace is doubled up upon itself, a soft unmuscled
somehow-living thing I remember that I love.

A premature sea-change; the pearls of your nails are blue,
your hair gone white, your body seaweed washed up on the shore.
We dry salt water that runs from you in rivulets.

11. PIE JESU

for Paddy McShane

SEMPITERNAM
REQUIEM

—'Tis a hard road.

—Aye.

—And, 'tis a soft.

—Aye, so it is.

—Best not to dwell on the spices of the sepulcher.

—Aye, nor the cauldron of the Crone.

—We each of us choose the boatman.

—Aye, and each the barge.

—For me a quicksilver ocean, and a faceful of spray.

—Aye, the company of dolphins and the lightening north.

For the sea is wide, and I cannot swim over
Nor have I wings that I could fly

12. IN PARADISUM

CHORUS ANGELORUM TE SUSCIPIAT
ET CUM LAZARO QUONDAM PAUPERE ÆTERNAM HABEAS REQUIEM

Every letter on the gravestone cost a fiver
but our hearts were set on Hamlet; 'Flights of Angels
Sing Thee to Thy Rest', from your favourite piece
by Tavener, in white on Kilkenny marble from the Black
Quarries at Arthur's Grove and Gallows Hill.

There is not enough space in Newry cemetery for the rate
of dying in the county, so a single plot these days has
to do for two. They dug the hole for you nine feet
deep to leave space for my father and I worry
that the roots of the flowers won't reach you.

It was a dark and narrow shaft to leave you at the bottom of.
Horses from the farm next door watched over the
chicken-wire fence and children from your first school
formed a guard of honour in maroon uniforms.
They would have been too young to have known you.

It's hard to get things from that time straight.
The headstone went up weeks afterwards. At first
there was just the fresh soil and a white wooden cross
and the yellow circle of your wedding ring we forgot
to take from your finger when they closed the box.

Weeping at the grave creates the song: Alleluia.

LIST OF QUOTATIONS

All Latin text is derived from the liturgical rite of the Catholic Mass for the dead, or Requiem Mass.

4. Tract: The French text is derived from 'J'ai perdu mon Eurydice', Orphée et Eurydice by Christoph Gluck.

9. Communion: The German text is from 'Mild und leise', Tristan und Isolde by Richard Wagner.

11. Pie Jesu: The quotation is from 'Carrickfergus', an Irish folk song.

12. In Paradisum: The quotation is from 'Song for Athene' by John Tavener.

TRANSLATION KEY

1. Introitus

Ad te omnis caro veniet .... To you all flesh shall come

2. Kyrie

Kyrie eleison .... Lord, have mercy on us
Christe eleison .... Christ, have mercy on us

3. Graduale

Requiem æternam dona eis, Domine ....
.... Grant them eternal rest, O Lord

4. Tract

Absolve, Domine, ...

animas omnium fidelium defunctorum ....

ab omni vinculo delictorum ....

.... Absolve, O Lord,

.... the souls of all the faithful departed

.... from every bond of sin.

Il a perdu son Eurydice .... He has lost his Eurydice

5. Sequentia

Dies iræ, dies illa .... Day of wrath, that day

Solvet sæclum in favilla, ... The world will dissolve in ashes

Teste David cum Sibylla .... Witnessed by David and the Sibyl.

6. Offertorium

Hostias et preces, tibi, Domine, laudis offerimus ....

.... Sacrifices and prayers, Lord, we offer you

7. Benedictus

Benedictus qui venit in nomine Domini! ....

.... Blessed is he who comes in the name of the Lord!

8. Agnus Dei

Agnus Dei qui tollis peccata mundi, ...

dona nobis pacem. ....

..... Lamb of God, who takes away the sins of the world,

.... grant us peace.

9. Communion

Lux perpetua luceat eis ...... Perpetual light shine upon them,
quia pius es .... because you are merciful

Seht ihr's nicht? ....
Immer lichter wie er leuchtet, ...
stern-umstrahlet hoch sich hebt? ....
.... Don't you see?
.... Brighter and brighter how he shines
.... Star-strewn, rising higher?

10. Libera me

Tremens factus sum ego, et timeo, ...
.... I am trembling and afraid
dum discussio venerit, atque ventura ira. ....
... Before the coming judgement, and the arriving wrath.

11. Pie Jesu

Sempiternam .... Everlasting
requiem .... rest

12. In Paradisum

Chorus angelorum te suscipiat ....
.... May the choir of angels greet you
et cum Lazaro quondam paupere æternam habeas requiem ...
and like Lazarus, who once was a poor man, may you have rest.

ACKNOWLEDGEMENTS

Selections from *Requiem* previously appeared in *Poetry Wales*, Spring 2017, Volume 52. I am grateful to my friends, my family, and all who have taught and continue to teach me. Particular thanks to Nia Davies, Tom McLaughlin, Malcolm Cocks, and Sean Bonney.

ABOUT THE POET

Based in Berlin, Síofra McSherry was born in Newry, Northern Ireland. She earned her PhD in American Literature from the Freie Universität Berlin in 2017. Síofra completed a BA English at the University of Oxford and received her MA from University College London. She has published her poems in anthologies including *The Salt Book of Younger Poets* (Salt, 2011), *Bird Book* (Sidekick Books, 2011), *Sylvia is Missing* (Flarestack, 2012) and journals including *Poetry Wales, Poems in Which, Foam:e, Abraxas* and *Hysteria*.

ABOUT THE ILLUSTRATOR

Emma Dai'an Wright is a British-Vietnamese publisher, designer and illustrator based in Birmingham, UK. She worked in ebook production at Orion Publishing Group before leaving in 2012 to set up the Emma Press with the support of the Prince's Trust.

THE EMMA PRESS
small press, big dreams

The Emma Press is an independent publisher dedicated to producing beautiful, thought-provoking books. It was founded in 2012 by Emma Dai'an Wright in Winnersh, UK, and is now based in Birmingham.

The Emma Press has been shortlisted for the Michael Marks Award for Poetry Pamphlet Publishers in 2014, 2015, 2016 and 2018, winning in 2016.

The Emma Press publishes themed poetry anthologies, single-author poetry and fiction chapbooks and books for children, with a growing list of translations.

The Emma Press is passionate about publishing literature which is welcoming and accessible. Sign up to the Emma Press newsletter to hear about upcoming events, publications and calls for submissions.

theemmapress.com
emmavalleypress.blogspot.co.uk